TURKISH V

First edition published in 2022 by Uitgeverij
An imprint of punctum books, Earth, Milky Way
https://www.punctumbooks.com

ISBN-13: 978-1-68571-092-7 (print)
ISBN-13: 978-1-68571-093-4 (ePDF)
DOI: 10.53288/0390.1.00
LCCN: 2022939164
Library of Congress Cataloging Data is available from the
Library of Congress

Book design: Vincent W.J. van Gerven Oei

spontaneous acts of scholarly combustion

MURAT NEMET-NEJAT

Turkish Voices

⋮

Contents

Dedicated to Cemal Süreya,
who drops the second "y" from his name

Turkish Voices

Paradise

Brooks of heaven flow,
Go chanting the divine name;
Birds, alive, curve, draw
Holy circles in a game.

Gentle trees glow in gold,
Their young roots disdain the earth,
Their hungry roots searching upwards
Wash down their thirst with Allah's name.

Older branches bend; ripe
With weight they understand,
Gently observe the red rose pray
Mad with perfumed flame.

New-born souls bite the tight-skinned fruit,
Smiles shine on them in gold;
They sip the outpoured juice, taste life's end,
Receive the clothes of Paradise.

Their fair faces round as the moon,
Their soft words fresh as the morn,
Wise Houri girls play among souls,
Ponder with them on Allah's name.

The soul which burns for the maker,
Its tears will flow like a river,
Its bones refine to a reed,
Chant His name with restrained greed.

Pir Sultan

The rough man entered the lover's garden
It is woods now, my beautiful one, it is woods,
Gathering roses, he has broken their stems
They are dry now, my beautiful one, they are dry

In this square our hide is stretched
Blesséd be, we saw our friend off to God
One day, too, black dust must cover us
We will rot, my beautiful one, we will rot

He himself reads and He also writes
God's holy hand has closed her crescent eyebrows
Your peers are wandering in Paradise
They are free, my beautiful one, they are free

Whatever religion you are, I'll worship it too
I will be torn off with you even the Day of Judgement
Bend for once, let me kiss you on your white neck
Just stay there for a moment, my beautiful one, just stay
    there

I'm Pir Sultan Abdal, I start from the root
I eat the kernel and throw out the evil weed
And weave from a thousand flowers to one hive honey
I am an honest bee, my beautiful one, an honest bee.

The woman stripped herself slowly,
Her shyness stripped her,
White and slowly
Without eye contact.

She didn't fetch her hair along,
Kept it on the dresser, full of despair;
But her hair fell through the unlit cracks,
I undid her drawers
I drowned myself in her hair.

She didn't bring her eyes along either,
So I only guessed her thoughts,
Her skin twitched
Like a rabbit's.

While a bypass
Is clearing
My upper plumbing,
A good lay
Is clearing
Her lower plumbing.

Muezzin

You hopped into bed,
But your hymen is on the table.
Never mind, Allah be praised.
There is more than one way to skin a cat.
Peel an orange and feed its slices to me.
I have a minaret, get hold of its charms,
Be my muezzin,
While the rain
Is pouring out in the street
And folks are keeping indoors
For their prayers.

The Bee

You are watching a bee whizzing by in the room
The way
You ate your milk pudding
Three days ago.

Only after mere three days of my cajoling,
Coaxing, feeding, lying
You reached this serenity:
Thin, naked
Your pale, still unripe breasts showing,
Leaning against the board,
Nibbling a mackintosh apple...

At night, the moon resurrects
The minarets,
Death flies with a somewhat beauty
Through hard, Koran-selling streets
(Death flies over child-soft faces),
I passed so many times
Through my streets
Your tongue's taste in my palate like sea-weeds,
Now misty, now blue-clear, now misty again
Like some sea-beings echoing some rabbits,
Echoing Mondays, echoing the other days,
Echoing Tuesday, Monday, Saturday and Wednesdays.

Drizzle

The stars were on the sidewalk
As if at the Prophet's coming
Because it had drizzled the night before
Dizzy like a cloud, I left her house
Skipping, skipping on the stars
Pleased as punch in the moonlight
Playing hopscotch
As at the Prophet's coming
Because it had drizzled the night before.

Houri's Rose

I'm crying exactly in the middle of the rose
As I die every evening in the middle of the street
Not knowing my front from my back in the dark
As I sense, I sense the receding of your eyes
Which prop me up.

I hold back your hands, kiss them in the night
Your hands are white, again white, again white,
I'm afraid that your hands are so white
That a caboose in the station somewhat
I'm late at the station sometime

Palming the rose I'm rubbing it on my face
Which Houri dropped in the street,
My arms are broken, my wings,
In a red, catastrophic music,
At the other end of the reed
A brand new, gold toothed shyster.

I can't bring myself;
When I can not resist her quinces and pomegranates
I bend my head
And walk away.
Nothing that wolves or birds can know.

Only I know
What bitch of a beauty I loved.
She has a mouth but no tongue -
The Fortress of Diyarbakır...

II.

The fertile plants bloom,
Blood red.
It snows on the other side.
The Black Mountain rocks
The Zozan rocks...
Look, my whiskers are frozen,
And I am cold
And the ice has grown longer and longer
And I'm thinking of you, as though you were spring,
Of you, as though you were Diyarbakır,
To what, to what isn't it superior
The taste of thinking of you...

I who am a master in the art of complaining,
I feed with my life these falcons of sadness,
You whose alchemy, gnarled, I grasp and lose in the crowd,
Your thin waist
Drumming from here, from there,
In your lands where once joyful banquets reigned
Now big beaks of lonely hours are circling,
Now, please, once again, begin to undress
From your mouth,
Loose, once again, all your beasts upon me,
Once again, come rising from your ruins,
Come to me, once again, and disperse me.

You were born
We kept you hungry
For three days,
We didn't give you your mother's nipples
Baby Adilosh
So you won't be sick
Because this is our custom,
Now attack the nipples,
Attack and grow...

These are
The rattlesnakes and scorpions
These have
Their eyes on our bread and food
Know them
Know them and grow
This is honor
Etched in our names
And this is patience
Seeped from oleanders
Grasp them
Grasp them and grow...

Whereas a glass of water was enough to wet your hair,
A slice of bread, two olives to fill our stomachs
If I kissed you once, the second felt itself neglected,
If I kissed you twice, the third bent its neck in sadness...

The Wall

The power
Power
Of seeing you
In pigtails
In pigtails,
The plain skirt
Of your school uniform
Around your hips,
Sweat
Against the wall
Against your wish
Against the wall
Against your wish.

Dorothy Lucy

Her eyes are not for seeing but an orchard for thieving
She's moving
From one room to another
Opening one door
She's closing another
Her name isn't Mary
But only Dorothy Lucy
Because of her color left without schooling
A jigger of nectar
Whispering
Her angry speeches
In my erogenous ear

Her pappy
Swinging
At his lynching party
She is so unhappy.

Dorothy Lucy's Lesson

Africa is still drawn the old way
On the maps
So the shape of the Mediterranean doesn't get spoiled.

Without Names

In The Flower Arcade
When I saw you first handle a glass of booze
I thought it apt to call you a flower,
Strung names of exotic flowers around you.

Now all those fantasies are gone!
Without names
The true pain starts now.

My hazel eyed beauty with the black mole
Do not misuse me as a stranger
Wind me round your waist
Like a golden shawl

It is in vain, my heart, all in vain
For the brave lad, death be delayed,
Take me to the tips of your hair
I'll weave like a thread

You, little girl, why don't you stand before me
Why don't you comprehend my state
Give me a lock of your hair
I'll smell it and crawl

Karacaoğlan says, what shall I do,
Lift your arms round my neck?
My coy delight let me be your subject
So you can use me like the floor

My home was a golden cage
With a friend's hand my heart is stabbed
I used to be near, now I'm far away
Someone took me from my coy delight

The plains of my friend are green with grass
With her sweet tongue she made me a promise
She used to swear that she wouldn't depart
Someone took me from my coy delight

Let me be muslin cloth and be torn for yards and yards
Let me be a slave bartered at the market place
My term isn't up yet, so how can I die and rest
Someone took me from my coy delight

Karacaoğlan says, be burnt and be used
Go, flow, mingle with the seas
Listen to a neighbor who suffered my loss
Someone took me from my coy delight

Seeing birds passing over you,
If I could break their wings...

Cutting a slice of watermelon to woo you,
I split my heart.

Pharaoh

The patron saint of the collectors.

What happened to the baby inside the sarcophagus

It shrivelled into a dream.

Dying in a Turkish Bath

Did you ever attend a public bath?
I did.
The candle near me blew out,
And I became blind.
The blue of the dome disappeared.

They relit a candle on the navel stone.
The marble was wiped clean.
I saw some of my face in it.
It was bad, something awful,
And I became blind.
I didn't expect quite this from my face.

Did you ever sob
While covered in soap?

The Yellow Heat

My breath is a red bird
In the yellow tide of your hair;
As I embrace you
Your legs grow long endlessly.

My breath is a red horse,
The burning on my cheeks tell me;
We are alone, our nights short,
Let us gallop together.

The most beautiful woman, she was,
She combed her hair, all of it pubic hair,
When she sat, she squatted,
A bloody woman, a horse of wind,
It kept occurring to me how deceptive she was.

Which of her parts most? Of course, her mouth.
Attuned to all the feelings,
An Alhambra of a mixture of kisses,
In the limitless sea of the sheets
Her tactile mouth went up and down.

Oh, my eyes, now,
Have begun a crying that keeps on going,
A woman's shirt is shrouding me,
The blue of the day is on that
The rooster of the night is in that.

I love your productive hands. So many.
Touching touching the lions the statue of lions.
Looms before us, so lovely, the statue of lions, of our
Love, superb statues of sadness, that is.

The clock chimed: hmmm.
Bending my brim hat over my misery,
Out of my white insomnia,
Exile to your face,
You woman,
You were in every dark corner,
Your ghost nettled on the dead street,
A child
Sang lullabies endlessly, and a viola de
Gamba lengthened the blue smile of a young mother,
And you insisted on my love for your thin beauty,
My hope, a contention in abyss.

A wife, a mother,
Who is she
So beautiful?
I looked
And looked.

Strike a match, your voice flamed in blue,
Through the bright trees, your voice, the sounds of your
    tongue,
Into my mouth you poured, thickly,
The secret thoughts
Of this dour-skinned, this upside-down, this strange
    passion,
In your poison-dripping forest, gasping,
I lived your short, terrifying reign,
My heart was entangled with the tide of your hair,
And mixed, wanting,
With the Bird Sea,
Then mixed with the Black Sea,
Then with wider waters.

Istanbul was half under the boat
A sixpack
Was hanging in the water.
"Let's row away,"
I told her.
She got up
To pick the oars,
Rocking the boat
Gently.
Being small boned
You'd think she could
Barely stand a kiss.

A lover possesses only his love,
And losing is harder than being lost,
Exile to your face, my woman!
I have not forgotten
Your eyes who are my brother,
Your forehead who is my child,
Your mouth who is my lover,
I have not forgotten your fingers
Who are my friends,
Your belly who is my wife,
Your front, your harlot's sides,
And your back,
And all these, all these, all these
I have not forgotten, how can I forget?

I had kissed you gently when I had kissed you first,
The boat was sailing along the shore,
Three breast strokes from the minarets,
Stretching
I had kissed you gently when I had kissed you first.

Through the transparent gown,
Low light from a table lamp in the back room,
Your long legs
Were luminous in the door.
I moved fearlessly.
Shame hung back
On the acacia trees
In the rain.
A muezzin was calling folks
To prayer.
We spread a picnic blanket
On the bed.
That's how everything happened first.

Look, now, the table
Has found its place;
When we were not here
Someone entered my room.

The wash is done,
Everything is ironed;
When I had left
This book was on the floor.

You couldn't drink from this bottle,
Its bottom was so mossy;
It's unbelievable,
This is another bottle.

This old ladle
Is clean now;
Fire is burning
In the stove, our lamp is burning.

I wanted to hop into bed right away.
A ghostly presence
Came over me the moment
I touched the bed of feathers.

My wife must have dropped in
When we were away.

Look, this is your loose thread of hair from last night,
This is the sagging bed,
No bullshit,
These sweet sheets wrinkled, twisted, full of stains...

To be the husband
Of my Leila
With the easy thighs
Isn't easy.

Dilnişin*

The child's bread roll is falling to the sea, what was I
    going to say?
Will all sorts of sea varmint race to the sesame seeds?
    Naturally.
It was stale anyway, hard and doughy, though the child
    liked it,
Won't fly off, don't worry, me grasping his leg. You're just
    like my own mother, dear!
Fine, you'll have your white dress with the blue flowers
    by fall.
As I was saying,
This granddad boat Dilnişin will have a hard time
Making it through to the next season.

* A shabby small boat running on the Bosphorus

You used to have a friend
About five years ago
I saw her yesterday
In the street. She was pleased.

Just there standing up
We said a few words.
She was married,
A girl and a boy.

She asked me about you.
"He hasn't changed a bit,"
I said. "As you knew him."
She understood.

She was happy. Loved her husband.
They owned their house now.
Like a criminal, guilty,
She sent you her regards.

Look, these are your hands, your feet, these,
So beautiful that they can't be any better
This is yourself, young stud, this width, this height.

Loving was such a panacea, a blood letting
That when it was raining on the Galata Bridge
The sky broke itself into two
And poured
Upon us.

Where your face ended and your body began,
That's to say your neck,
Was an erogenous, neutral zone,
The slippery cliff of passion.

Toes,
Toes,
Without
Shoes,
Oh, my darling!

Sitting on the Face

The part of her body I don't remember
Is the face.

Objects

Talcum powder, squat vaseline jar,
A queen bed
Always covered with a bed spread,
Humiliation
Visible in the ceiling mirror.

Left foot
Behind the ankle,
You shy
Icon.

But I know
The shades
Of whip marks
On your back.
You smeared
Rouge
On your cheeks.
I smeared
Rouge
On your ass.

In that motel
In Jamaica
A converted
Old
Plantation.

"The blue spots inside my thighs
That you gave me are patches
Of honor," you told me.
I was thrilled,
But I also believed
That the black and blue spots on your ass
Were there because
You fell off a horse.

Allah be praised, the color of flowers
Is creeping up again.

A hermaphrodite, she makes love biting his own lip.

A stalk outbursts in miniature a city,
Down this stalk, round these streets, I press for you,
The world curbing circles, leaf by leaf, around you,
All thoughts of gold, the gilded coins,
And the right to press these coins,
The Euphrates,
And its sister river merging,
Dark circles in my eyes,
Trees of Babylon sapping,
The Sea of Marmara,
And the monsters in that water,
The sea crabs,
The land crabs, the sand crabs, the louse crabs,
Circling love crabs, the hermits, stoned barnacles,
Begonias, irises, castanets, all make towards you.

In Turkey at least
Masturbation brings acne.
Up to an age it also intensifies heartache, longing
Though it heals longing
After a certain age.

Neither the sick wait for morning
Nor the tree for the martyr
Nor Satan for sin
As I wait for you

You dropped your shadow in my dreams
In my wet dreams
I drenched you
Now you may not return,
If you will.

Trucks carry melons;
I think always of her;
Trucks carry melons;
I think always of her;

When the world changes,
Different water, different weather, different soil;
When the world changes,
Different water, different weather, different soil;

This city is different, I see;
Everybody fooled me;
This city is different, I see;
Everybody fooled me.

Trucks carry melons;
I think always of her;
Trucks carry melons;
I think always of her.

A street walker is giving him a broken tipped sword,
    reveals herself on the rung of a ladder.
Oh, Benjamin!

Two snakes entwined, trajectories melting away at an
    inn.
Oh, Benjamin!

Kneeling, he groans, weaned off the smell of armpits.
Oh, Benjamin!

A cup of hemlock kept out of reach against the
    possibility of drink.
Oh, Benjamin!

A fortress tower rings, of eunuchs, washed in the flood.
Oh, Benjamin!

He is combing his hair in cum, then treated to flowers.

What is this lad doing in Istanbul, banged about by an agitation which is after the knowledge of knives?

He is showing off his pompadour, then, face downward, disappearing among the flight of birds in the plains of Tirnova.

He is an inveterate, a pervert. Such talk about him. He doesn't go near women as he should, an erect plume on his head, a pornographic masterpiece.

He is buried alive in the ground. Head first. Ouch!

How did it get stuck to him, this wedding gift, and the bride's golden threads in his hair all over the place?

A few colors explain everything: a crystal ball breeding a pure black, a red bird singing with a swollen throat. Hoot hoot.

To find Turkey is easy
Turkey is the palm of your hand
But you should tell its true name to no one
Believe me they will laugh at you.

At the courtyard of the Blue Mosque, a secret ritual. The muezzin is turning the pages of the sultan's private book woven with naked slaves, whipping time to shreds.

In a division of labor, bushy commanders and dreamy slaves join, tearing to pieces during the riotous orgies, the pages of the Orthodoxal,* revealing their reveries.

A mistiness after the rain, hammered with pain.

He dreams a crooked spell, a diagonal, so so paradise.

Found out, the commander's tunic is ripped off, his gold epaulets are ripped off. His slaves escape giggling.

Now, a bag man, accosting and being teased by foundlings.

* The Holy Book of Orthodox Christianity.

He got in backdoors, my pasha, a proud prisoner with a moustache. Kneeling he did his own daughter.

And with an axe he let loose on merry pipes. Lifted the crinoline skirt of a lady.

Reaching the beads of prayer round her neck, he reared. When groin to groin, a sea of imploration, a street singer.

Making arches, yells continued under the dome. Because of a tight underpinning of dress, in her pride, she couldn't confess.

Though he had three of his fingers chopped, he was too strong for her.

Oh, play on, the squid's ink music!

He's in the numberless arms of his mother, a new self-sufficiency. He faces death with a wide brow, faces it accepting it. On her bosom, in a tub, the color of forget-me-nots. Winds of Vernal Equinox blow from Mitsrayim. Hot winds, forty days. They bathe in his loneliness.

They sheared the cloud, the cloud now is clear;
My blood spills on the ground, the cloud is modest,
Blushes
And disappears.

A man's face shadows
In my palm;
I see it and squeeze it,
Drinking stars
From the urinal.

In a testy mood
The same mood that
Tore me apart.

His face is almost gone,
My desolation is pure,
The water is flat,
My pain is on.

Easy
Like drinking from
The tap water.

When minarets
Are at the train window
In Erzurum,
Drinking tea
Reminds me of you
Darling.

No no no
Go.
You Baluchi farmer
Donkey
Dresser
Henna mixer
Donkey fucker
You gorgeous you
Donkey fucker
Bead stringer
Talisman kisser
Baluchi farmer
Donkey fucker
Henna mixer
You
Gorgeous
You
Baluchi farmer
Koran reader
Donkey fucker...

It is the age, I can't resist it,
It is the age of your most
Intricate, rebellious, hell-budding
Body.
It is the age, forty nights and forty days
Your arms noosed around my neck,
And my heart, bent on evil...
What can I say?
When military patrols crush our sleep,
My heart is taken by you...
Your shadow even
Is forbidden on water pools.

I am a spinning wheel
A weeping water mill
Pining to kill
Love's infidel chill
The falcon's cruel bill
Pecking me is a thrill
Love brooding on my window sill
Tears pouring down a hill

I can not come down though your garden is in plunder,
My knife becomes as bright as hell,
Then you come down on me,
My hands are all broken...

In your secret, most private parts traps are set.
Some days I see you give up
The corrupting love of this world.
Some days,
You may fall.
Don't fall
Without me,
I will die...
I will miss your eyes, your eyes.

My black mulberry, my forked darky, my Gypsy,
My grain of pomegranate, my grain of light, my only
    one;
I am a tree, my limbs, a porch hanging with grapes,
I am a hive, you are my honey, my bitter honey,
My sin, my ague.

Tongue of coral, teeth of coral, thighs of oyster,
I gave you a life, my wife,
My black mulberry, my forked darky, my Gypsy,
What more will you be to me, my odd one, queer one,
My smiling quince, my weeping pomegranate,
My baby, my stallion, my wife.

When quinces become pomegranates
You become mine,
When above our troubled heads
The world is translucent.

The Apple

You are eating an apple stripped naked
And the apple is an apple, nature's bounty,
One side of it red, the other side also red,
Birds are flying over you
There is a sky over your head
If I can remember it, you stripped yourself exactly three
    days ago,
On a wall,
On the one side, you are eating an apple, red,
On the other side, you are giving away your love for free,
    warm,
A wall in Istanbul.

I'm also naked but I'm not eating an apple
I have lost all appetite for such apples,
I saw too many apples, you can't believe it,
Birds are on my head, these are birds after your apple
There is sky on my head, this is the sky in your apple,
If I can remember it, we stripped ourselves together,
On a church,
On the one hand, I am tolling a bell to full living
On the other hand, people are passing in the street as a
    mob
On a church wall

A wall in Istanbul, a church wall
You are eating an apple stripped naked

You are eating an apple to the middle of the sea
You are eating an apple to the middle of my heart
On the one hand, our youths are in a profound sadness
On the other hand, the Sirkeci train terminal are full of
    men and women and children
Accustomed to letting only their mouths be kissed
Instead of doing their business standing up

I am dropping one letter from my name
The pimp dropping hints on the other side of the
    doorway.

I can't protect the sadness of my labia,
Its silver wings.

I was drunk,
Swallowing the cum
Good to the last drop,
hey!
Shitdiggers in my hand,
Splashing through the rain,
Holding a parasol.
An old hag, I am,
A worthless student of lust,
Once caught with my bearded pasha
With a whip.

The cobble stoned avenues of Istanbul are involved in
    their expiration,
Expiated.
Only the snows are left behind,
Then the rains come.

Oh, dear Istanbul, my main drag,
No one can console me, how can one,
Oh, oh,
My mouth is receding, my azure eyes.

With a bazooka I am shooting at the pictures of
    desolation,
The centerfold leaves of an underground magazine.

Bury my wounded song
Under a penny laid on your eyes;
Listen, I won't be long!

You did me wrong,
But a lover can't complain when love dies;
Bury my wounded song;

I will quietly bite my tongue,
Stop reliving ancient, poisoned tales;
Listen, I won't be long!

Swearing to be strong
I sever forever our ties
Though I feel like a worm;
Bury my wounded song.

Just hush along,
May you one day
In the earth try your size;
Wait, wait a minute, I won't be long!

If one day another worm
Plays music on your thighs...
Plays music on your thighs...

But I said, I said, I won't be long,
Bury my wounded song.

A Virtuous Lady's Unfortunate Life

His name was Rüştü Pasha, was called Mad Rüştü in the
    Ottoman Army
Hamit was the Sultan then, his moustache long, long,

He had a beard, perhaps he was merely a beard,
Perhaps behind the beard a forest of a man

And the ships, like this, up the Bosphorus, down,
My husband pasha twisted his moustache, without
    giving a damn

Everything flew by then, and we were so surprised
Freedom, then the parliament, then the thirty-first of
    March, then...

My sleep is fragments, I only wait for a call
You tell me, wise owl, when is dying coming, when...

I always looked up to something, defended it, was a girl
He was angry, had a harem, had a beard, he was my
    husband then

I remember one night at the top of the hill
Your weighty horses were Hungarian, my lace German

The naval chief Tevfik Pasha, the armistice, and Allah
    knows what else
How the world withdrew from under my feet then

A daughter, a son, two brides, one groom, Zurich,
    Lausanne,
How I cried after our house burned

I had not died yet, with my August and my pearls,
Before the night we visited our villa under a fulllit moon

When does my flower fade, when does the water, when
    the night
When were the ships, when my pasha husband, then...

Now only my aged glory could ease the glare of a
    chandelier
Tell me, the nights in my villa, when is Wise Death
    coming, when...

Elegies are read, waves wake behind a ship's stern
I am dead, Mrs. Chastity, from virtue's burn

A watermelon broke,
The boy nudging it
(Because
Rounder?)
From under the pile.
Like a panicked crab
The watermelon slipped
Round the edge
Of the cart,
Which was infinitesimally
Tilted.
His eyes
Opened in shock.

Trinkets and Other Attic Secrets

A crib-death deserted in the lobby of the mosque. The hermaphrodite ma, till last month my pa's helter-skelter empress, is spreading the lilies of repentance on an anonymous burial ground.

They always hide the disaster in the attic of an empty villa.

My Aunt Sadness drinks alcohol in the attic, embroiders,

Bent over, weeping,
Her neurons nuked out,
A hunchback in atonement,
Singing, singing moody, mournful

Perverse directives in villanelles,
Spun like a gossamer
Among the breezy cordage,
By Barbarossa,
Then her only sea captain,
Once her slave.

Punishment Fit the Crime

They maroon the virulent Penis in a rubber room,
Shuffling there the elusive floors endlessly,
Kept straight
In a straight jacket.

I, in my room overlooking the seashore,
Not looking out of the window,
Know that the boats sailing out in the sea
Go loaded with watermelons.

Multiplication of Passion in a Cursed Triangle

Death is a drop of passion
Seen from another angle
Seen from another angle
Seen.

Peeping Tom

The woman
Passing the soap
Along the
Curves of her body,
One leg up;
The soap appears
And disappears.

What likes ice cream, sex and lives in a dark place?
Tongue.

Gazel

With such eyes, with such sea, with such gazel,
With such illness I saw you, with such illness I knew you,
    with such illness I lived you

However good, however lovely, however ugly you were,
However honest your husband was, finally, you were a
    rose on a live wire

An i.o.u. peddled in an Assyrian War
A satrap's shyster trick claiming our bread, our chore

You were the finest Indian muslin spun like a Sophist's
    logic,
I, a porcupine addicted to a peacock

Exhausting you was my obsessive dream
A mute, interior, intimate scream

In this scream, in this muteness, in this gazel,
With this dream I wept over you, with this scream I
    hoped for you, in this dream I prayed to you

Turkish Voices, Afterthoughts

I. Fragments at the Beginning of a Poetic Journey

Turkish Voices, written during 1989/90, is initially based on the *Second New* Turkish poet Cemal Süreya's first book of poetry, *Üvercinka (Pigeon English),* which he wrote during the 1950s, in his twenties.[1] In this book, absolutely stunning erotic passages of uncanny psychological insight, where a nexus between pleasure and power is revealed through the lyric persona of a male seducer, are mixed with cute refrains or half-digested surrealist lines which blur the text, sentimentalizing that insight by turning the poems into general appeals for freedom, completely overlooking the victimization of the female persona, who never speaks. I decided to see what would happen to this book, which I loved, if I eliminated all the passages I considered weak from it. In the ensuing experiment, which lasted about a year, fragments from different poems in the book, sometimes ending in mid-sentence, began to be isolated and spliced together; then, a few underwent alterations; then, fragments from other Turkish poets entered the melee, splitting the lyric persona, opening up its unity; finally, poems written by me earlier joined the text. The result is a series of eighty-four fragments where any idea of ownership or originality or source - what poem, that is, comes from whom or where - disappears, blurring any

1   *Üvercinka* was published in 1958. *The Second New* was a poetry movement in Turkey whose heyday lasted about twenty years, from the fifties into the early seventies.

boundaries. In other words, what starts with the ego and power-centered persona of the male seducer is dissolved, splintered, through a dialectic or critical confrontation with Süreya's resistant text, into multiple points of view, often of a sufferer, a victim. What one ends up with is a multiplicity of voices, an erotic poem which becomes its own critique of power.

In retrospect, myself being completely unaware of it at the time, *Turkish Voices* turned out to be, in key aspects, a pivotal work in my development as a poet, a translator, and a thinker on poetics, on the arts, and on their relationships across different media – a development that did not bear its first concrete, discernible fruit until ten years later. The first occurred in the approach I took in *Eda: An Anthology of Contemporary Turkish Poetry,* published in 2004, which I edited and in which I did most of the translations and wrote the majority of the essays.[2] Here is how my introduction to *Eda,* "The Idea of a Book," starts:

> As much as a collection of translations of poems and essays, this book is a translation of a language. Due to the fortuitous convergence of historical, linguistic and geographic factors, in the 20th century – from the creation of the Turkish Republic in the 1920's to the 1990's when Istanbul/Constantinople/Byzantium turned from a jewel-like city of contrasts of under a million to a city of twelve million – Turkey created a body of poetry unique in the 20th century, with its own poetics, world view and idiosyncratic sensibility. What is more these qualities are intimately related to the nature of Turkish

2   Murat Nemet-Nejat, ed., *Eda: An Anthology of Contempory Turkish Poetry* (Jersey City: Talisman House, 2004).

as a language – its strengths and its defining limits. As historical changes occurred, the language in this poetry responded to them, flowered, changed; but always remaining a continuum, a psychic essence, a dialectic which is an arabesque. It is this silent melody of the mind – the cadence of its total allure – which this collection tries to translate. While every effort has been made to create the individual music of each poem and poet, none can really be understood without responding to the movement running through them, through Turkish in the 20th century. I call this essence *eda*, each poet, poem being a specific case of eda, unique stations in the progress of the Turkish soul, language.

In *The Task of the Translator* Walter Benjamin says that what gives a language "translatability" is its distance from the host language. *Eda* is this distance.[3]

This is what my dialectical response – more a confrontation – with Cemal Süreya's mysterious text was leading to: a reorientation from the concept of poetry as consisting of individual poem-units, attached to distinct poets' names, to a focus on the totality of a language. Freed from biography or even individual dreams, this poetry that is led and shaped by dynamic, impersonal forces driving its language – tapping its grammar/magma – will truly be the voice of the people that produced it. Bypassing official platitudes, it will be more intimately ("under the radar" so to speak) attuned to the cultural and political forces of the place in

3   Murat Nemet-Nejat, "The Idea of a Book," in ibid., 4.

which it was *imagined* – its silenced voices, their *"silent melody of the mind/soul."*

In *Eda*, the poetics the Turkish anthology sets up, the erotic and spiritual, personal and political join in a fluid multi-directional continuum. Tissues of thought infuse the body of language – in an audio-visual space where each poem is part of a greater linguistic whole.

II. The Broken Jar, Thoughts on Walter Benjamin's Idea of Translation

In an address on Walter Benjamin and his relation to the American poet Jack Spicer I gave at Stevens Institute in 1999, I describe translation as the anarchic form of our time:

> I want to discuss translation, not as an auxiliary activity in literature; but as an independent genre, like the lyric or the epic, with a distinct ethos and mode of thinking. I'll conceive of translation as the anarchic poetic form of our time.[4]

In that essay I imply that Benjamin's concept of pure language (*intentio*) in "The Task of the Translator" represents an explosive new poetic direction arrived at by re-defining the concept of translation. Translation ceases to be a movement from A to B, a bridging of distance framed by the idea of faithfulness to an original totality, in various degrees always doomed to failure,[5] words always remaining imprisoned within their *modes of intention*. Instead, A and B move to C, a space of synthesis,[6] where meaning (a

---

4   Murat Nemet-Nejat, "Translation: Contemplating against the Grain (A Talk on Walter Benjamin Given at Stevens Institute in 1999)," *Cipher Journal*, https://www.cipherjournal.com/html/nemet-nejat_spicer.html.

5   *Traduttore, traditore.*

6   Benjamin calls it "a place of harmony of all": "The Task of the Translator," in *Illuminations: Essays and Reflections*, trans. Harry Zorn, ed. Hannah Arendt (New York: Schocken Books, 1969), 74.

defined mode) is replaced by potential meaning, intentio, the impulse of words to crack open their modes of intention and mutate, etching an ever flowering replica of the human consciousness across time and space:

Cause and Effect, a Linguistic Play:
the Metaphysics of a Poem

"We think words are for us, we're for them."

While

in our daily life cause precedes effect ("Nothing comes of nothing"), i.e., cause is the cause of effect–they're the same. In language a new meaning is its own cause (*because of effect*), effect *imagines* cause, it is the original cause of effect. In the mirror of language one experiences the world upside down, time is reversed (or, paralyzed, time frees itself and dissolves into air...). We see the future as the past. Etymologically, each word has infinite openings lying **be**-fore it. But once a direction is taken, just at that moment language materializes a new meaning for that sound and instantly another infinity opens around the word (as if expanding waves around a pebble, or Basho's frog, casting itself into the water). Time in language's built by a series of instantaneous transformations that while we imagine that the old meaning is the builder of this home, its original cause, a brick. Whereas what we have is endless expansion, tracing the motions of endless soul. Whereas the cause is just a whim, a stirring of the wind, occurring that instant, *Not Necessary*. Absolutely necessary in the ocean of the imagination, of which words are just waves, meaning is just what we can see, looking into the darkness of ourselves, into its infinite dangers and riches in which we are a momentary dream, surrounded by dreams. What we call universe, what we call language.

A selfie depicting oblivion surrounds the individual dream into which I wake.... I dream I'm wading. [7]

An etymological dictionary, depicting the movement of roots across languages and time, incarnating different *modes of intention* – unstable and true only for that instant of time and place – is the closest replica in words of Benjamin's "pure language." Such a dictionary is, in essence, an anthology of "transparent translations"[8] among multiple times and languages.

*

In subtle (or not so subtle) put-downs, positivists describe Benjamin's thoughts on "pure language" as "mystical" or "poetic." Nothing can be further away from the truth. Benjamin is imagining (in terms of his "dialectical history," *dreaming*[9]) a poetry of the future that integrates the revolutionary changes occurring in physics of his time with quantum mechanics.

7   Murat Nemet-Nejat, *Io's Song* (Tucson: Chax Press, 2019), 88.
8   Benjamin calls the space ("arcade") that translation creates transparent.
9   The way the plethora of shops and goods in the Parisian arcades is dreaming the virtual world wide world.

Benjamin imagines in pure language a hypertext of infinity – an arcade: "if the sentence is the *wall* before the language of the original, literalness is the arcade"[10] – a space where temporal logical correspondences among words are replaced by quantum jumps, echoes, tangential frictions, and relations among fragments, misreadings – all possible, all legitimate in that new mathematical space. A poetry of the mind – of expansive/expanding consciousness – is created, a vision of the infinity of the spirit:

the bee precedes colors into a bouquet of flowers.[11]

    suicide

the fly hits the mirror

&

vanishes

into its dream

                (within *this* dream)[12]

Mental structures's authority is attacked in an anarchic act of liberation. The non-existent and existent become one: the *act* (*ual*) being a small subset of the poetic energy of *potent* (*ial*):

10 Benjamin, "The Task of the Translator," 79. My emphasis.
11 Camels & Weasels, unpublished manuscript.
12 Ibid.

Cinéma Vérité: Zombie

non-existing, being a state of being—
it appears

in the
film reel.

god is that *bee ing*, whose essence is nonexisting.

in her last forbidden caresses

a-weeping

dream-
boat,

sleek
like otters
fresh
out of water

streaking

oh,
dripping

on my sighs![13]

13 Murat Nemet-Nejat, *Animals of Dawn* (Northfield: Talisman House, 2016), 16.

Fragments of a vessel [...] need not to be like another [...] as fragments of a greater language..."[14]

*

In Benjamin's transparent translation, the clarity of meaning is replaced by a blur. This occurs because, Benjamin implies, in such translation the grammatical system of one language is imposed on another, creating both chaotic and transformative holes ("arcades"),[15] in the shape of mismatches, tangential openings. As a result, the language thins, its syntactical sinews weaken, semantic relationships (and certainties) melt into jumps, echoes – cracks, portals (quantum holes!) through which light, i.e., the *mind's eye,* can enter and get hold of poetic language:

a translation, instead of resembling the meaning of the original, must lovingly and in detail *incorporate* the

---

14 Benjamin, "The Task of the Translator," 78. My emphasis.
15 This is the underlying meaning of the paradoxical, seemingly contradictory statement in "The Task of the Translator": "if the sentence is the wall before the language of the original, literalness is the arcade" (79). The sentence embodies syntax, therefore, is part of the *mode of intention* of the language, whereas "literalness" applies to words. "In the beginning was...." Words precede syntax, are distinct units. Detaching themselves from the syntax, they may *play* freely among themselves, cracking into fragments, and fragments through tangential, frictional relations creating syntactical/spiritual holes – as a result, stretching, extending, subverting the sinews of the syntax, pulling it into the gravity of their field of interaction. That verbal field, each word/fragment with its gravitational mass, is the arcade. That is the reason for the astral glow.

It is interesting to me that in *The Arcades Project* Benjamin devotes long passages to the anarchist Ricardo's feverish writings on the cosmos.

original's mode of signification [its alien syntax], thus making both the original and the translation recognizable as fragments of a greater language, just as fragments are part of a vessel.[16]

Infinite as memory: forgetfulness

    Hummingbird

Before we part   did
A moment we share together
you having placed a small nutrient vial of translucent liquid
                                       on your porch
and I, watching birds dipping into them
you away,
        in instantaneous darts.

Do you remember?[17]

*

In essence, Benjamin is reversing God's act at The Tower of Babel in the Old Testament. Within the Jewish context this is a rebellious act, insisting on bringing to the surface the light of a spiritual unity that God suppresses, does not permit ("Thou shalt not eat of the fruit of the tree of knowledge"). It is a Promethean poetic act. Paradoxically, Benjamin's poetic vision of unity leads to a broken jar – flawed, open-ended, loose-fitting, rather than perfect and immutable. "The Task of the Translator" is a poetics

16   Benjamin, "The Task of the Translator," 78. Emphasis mine.
17   Nemet-Nejat, *Animals of Dawn*, 55.

of freedom – of anarchic break and rejuvenation – words *thinning* to their essences, in the ear and to the eye, basically occurring in consciousness (the "objective" world only a subset of it), their meaning resonating in the mind (and in the soul).

In "The Task of the Translator" and his later work, Benjamin opens the door to a poetics by which what has been by social modes of thought silenced becomes visible. And silence, instead of being a suppression, a lack, a state of abject enslavement, is ionized into a utopian vision of potentiality, psychic potency.

Silence gains its peculiar sound in space. As a result, the poem assumes a new visual dimension, ideally becoming a film montage with words – which keep gaining new *modes of intention,* which remain so only for an instant, in dreamlike echoes in the peripheries of the mind and cosmos, moving in all directions of the screen:

Burial of What Isseen in Silen c[18]

 r r

e   go   d[19]

            o

          o   scape

     o[20]

18 Murat Nemet-Nejat, *The Spiritual Life of Replicants* (Greenfield: Talisman House, 2011), 3.
19 Ibid., 50.
20 Ibid., 34. *The Spiritual Life of Replicants* is part IV of a seven-part

To set free in his own language the pure language *spell-bound* in the foreign language, to liberate the language imprisoned in the work by rewriting it, is the translator's task.[21]

The poem ceases to be a signifying agent ("No poet writes for others," Benjamin says). Instead, the signified as "symbolized *thing*"[22] – visible sound, as transparent translation – penetrates the very sinews of language.

Tangentially, in thinned filaments of language, the signifier gains the sanctity of an ever elusive substance, which Benjamin calls "the truth."[23]

Murat Nemet-Nejat
May 2, 2022

poem *The Structure of Escape.*

21 Walter Benjamin, "The Translator's Task," trans. Steven Rendall, *TTR* 10, no. 2 (1997): 163. My emphasis.

22 Benjamin, "The Task of the Translator," 79. Emphasis mine.

23 Ibid., 77.

Made in the USA
Middletown, DE
04 July 2022

68195647R00070